The Battle of BENTONVILLE

Illustrated With Maps, Engravings, And Photographs

by
Weymouth T. Jordan, Jr.

BROADFOOT PUBLISHING COMPANY
Wilmington, North Carolina
1995

"Fine Books Since 1970."

BROADFOOT PUBLISHING COMPANY

1907 Buena Vista Circle

Wilmington, North Carolina 28405

THIS BOOK IS PRINTED ON ACID-FREE PAPER

ISBN NO. 1-56837-004-0

ACKNOWLEDGMENTS

This booklet was produced with the generous assistance of Erik France of the Perkins Library, Duke University, and Torrey McLean of the State Records Center, North Carolina Division of Archives and History. Mr. France is a long-time student of the Battle of Bentonville who has uncovered an impressive amount of new material on the battle and elucidated it considerably beyond the work of earlier historians. Much of what has been written about Bentonville during the past ten years was founded on his yet unpublished research. Mr. McLean is the author of a remarkable series of fifteen unpublished maps (from which the maps in this booklet were adapted) detailing the movements of the two armies during the battle — at some stages on an hourly basis. I am grateful to both of these fine historians for allowing me access to their work and for critiquing my manuscript. I believe that they have never received the credit they deserve for their pioneering research on Bentonville, and it is a pleasure to acknowledge them both for the excellence of their scholarship.

I am also grateful to Greg Mast, an unattached scholar whose encyclopedic knowledge of North Carolina's role in the Civil War never fails to amaze me; to Richard Knapp of the Historic Sites Section, North Carolina Division of Archives and History; and to Jack Rose and Johnny Goode, site manager and assistant site manager at the Bentonville Battleground State Historic Site, for their careful reviews of my manuscript. Trudy Rayfield and Lisa Bailey of the Historical Publications Section, North Carolina Division of Archives and History, provided proofreading expertise as did my mother, Mrs. Louise Jordan, of Greenville, North Carolina, who was a professional proofreader and editorial assistant prior to her retirement. These readers made suggestions for improvements, ferreted out inconsistencies, and detected factual, interpretive, and technical errors. My sincere thanks to them all.

Weymouth T. Jordan, Jr.
Raleigh, 23 November 1989

TABLE OF CONTENTS

LIST OF MAPS

—1—

North Carolina in March, 1865

War and invasion were not new to North Carolina when General Sherman's victorious army, fresh from its devastating march through Georgia and South Carolina, crossed into the state near Laurel Hill in early March, 1865. The Outer Banks and such coastal plain towns as New Bern, Washington, and Plymouth had been occupied by Federal forces as early as 1861 and 1862. Winton and Pollocksville, also in the east, had been put to the torch, and the vital port of Wilmington had been seized after a bloody battle at Fort Fisher in January, 1865. Much of the eastern third of the state, from a line running from Wilmington through Goldsboro to Weldon, had been laid waste in fighting between Confederate forces and Union raiders operating out of New Bern or other bases. Particularly destructive were Federal irregulars known as "Buffaloes" and their Confederate counterparts, called "Partisan Rangers," who looted, burned, and murdered with bandit-like abandon. Under these conditions, thousands of terrorized and destitute inhabitants of the no-man's-land between the zones of Federal and Confederate control fled their homes for safer areas. Long before the arrival of General Sherman, whose theories of "Total War" had been thoroughly implemented in Georgia and South Carolina, much of the eastern third of North Carolina had become a region of ruin and desolation.

In the North Carolina mountains, where pro-Union sentiment was strong, Federal raids from East Tennessee had occurred, but a "dirty war" pitting Confederate regulars and home guardsmen against Unionist guerrillas and Confederate deserters was the true order of the day. Lynchings, bushwhackings, and quasi-legal executions were commonplace, sparking vendettas that widened the circle of violence and savagery. Confederate authority was so weak that several counties were virtually under deserter control.

The central part of the state, known as the piedmont, over which the shadow of Sherman's army now began to fall, had been spared some of the horrors visited upon the mountains and coastal plain, but scores of woods and creek valleys were the refuge of deserters on the run from Confederate home guardsmen. In the piedmont, as elsewhere, shortages of many necessities of life, valueless currency, the general lawlessness occasioned by war, and the absence or deaths of husbands, fathers, and sons had reduced the long-suffering civilian population to a condition approaching abject misery. This war-weariness, now turning to despair as Sherman approached, further undermined morale in the battered army of General Joseph E. Johnston that would attempt to defend the state. Even so, there was fight left in this much-defeated command. Although Robert E. Lee would surrender the Army of Northern Virginia at Appomattox Court House in early April and Johnston would surrender his own force scarcely two weeks later, most Confederate leaders and thousands of Confederate soldiers were not yet ready to admit that their cause was lost. Marshaling his rag-tag army and laying plans to trap the numerically superior but perhaps overconfident hosts of Sherman, Johnston prepared to make a stand.

JOSEPH E. JOHNSTON

—2—

The Confederate Commander — Joseph E. Johnston

Joseph Eggleston Johnston was an experienced and respected professional soldier who had acquired a reputation for ability and personal bravery as long ago as the Seminole and Mexican wars. Somewhat below middle height and slight of build, he was a man of unpredictable temperament but possessed sound judgment, a certain jaunty elegance, and an air of calm resolution that inspired confidence and made him a natural leader. Now 58 years old, he was outranked in 1865 by only one other Confederate field general, his fellow Virginian and former West Point classmate Robert E. Lee.

Johnston's Civil War career began in July, 1861, at First Manassas (known in the North as First Bull Run), where he shared command with P. G. T. Beauregard and helped win one of the South's greatest victories. The following May he was wounded in the chest and shoulder near Seven Pines, southeast of Richmond, while opposing the advance of a gargantuan Federal army under George B. McClellan. Recovered from his wounds, he was assigned to the West where he failed, under difficult if not impossible circumstances, to relieve the doomed Confederate fortress at Vicksburg. In December, 1863, he was given command of the Army of Tennessee, which had just been defeated at Chattanooga and driven into North Georgia. Instructed to take the offensive against the superior Federal army, now commanded by Sherman, Johnston was instead flanked out of one defensive position after another. By the summer of 1864, following numerous futile attempts to lure his illusive opponent into battle on disadvantageous terms, Johnston had fallen back to the gates of Atlanta. Confederate President Jefferson Davis, convinced that nothing could be expected from a general whom he regarded as a "retreat specialist," then sacked Johnston and replaced him in July, 1864, with the combative but impetuous John B. Hood. When Sherman captured Atlanta in September, Hood, hoping to draw the Federal army after him, moved north to attack Sherman's supply line to Tennessee. Detaching General George H. Thomas to deal with Hood, Sherman set out southeastward with about 60,000 men on his "March to the Sea." At Franklin and Nashville, in November and December, 1864, the Army of Tennessee was badly mauled by Thomas. Hood resigned a few weeks later. In February of the new year Johnston was dispatched to South Carolina to take command of the remnants of his former army. His assignment was the same one he had been unable to accomplish in Georgia in 1864: Stop Sherman.

It seems unlikely in retrospect that anything short of divine intervention could have stopped Sherman in March, 1865, but Johnston was perhaps the best choice possible for an impossible job. He had an intimate if painfully acquired knowledge of his opponent, he was a leader and tactician of superior ability, and he retained the confidence of Lee, the Confederate general-in-chief. More importantly, the men in the ranks would fight for him. Many of these tough, weary veterans had served under Johnston; others knew him by reputation. He had never abused the courage of his men or sacrificed them rashly, as Hood had done. They did not believe that he would do so. This conviction was very significant. It eliminated one possible motivation for desertion and provided some assurance that Johnston would have what he would need most to defeat Sherman — an army.

Johnston accepted his new assignment with reluctance. It was too late, he believed, to defeat Sherman. Nevertheless, he had orders to do so and intended to try. To have a chance he would need to concentrate his badly scattered command, he would need to attack the Federal army one isolated segment at a time, and he would need the element of surprise. Federal complacency should also work in his favor. Sherman had not encountered serious opposition since he marched out of Atlanta almost four months ago, and he would not be expecting it now.

THE BATTLEFIELD OF FRANKLIN, TENNESSEE. FROM A PHOTOGRAPH.

WILLIAM T. SHERMAN

—3—

The Federal Commander — William T. Sherman

William Tecumseh Sherman has been described, along with Grant and Thomas, as one of the three generals who won the war for the Union. Few historians would dispute Sherman's inclusion in that triumvirate, but his rise to prominence probably owed no more to his merit as a commander than to his political connections, which included his brother John in the U.S. Senate and his friendship with two generals — Grant and Henry W. Halleck — who were in a position to advance his career. Almost certainly, the red-headed Ohioan's erratic early-war performance on and off the battlefield would have terminated the career of any officer unblessed with his powerful sponsors.

Sherman made his Civil War debut at First Manassas, where his brigade was caught up in the great rout of the Federal army. Although he hardly distinguished himself, he kept his head, was among the last to leave the field, and, in other respects, demonstrated somewhat more sense and competence than his maladroit superiors. Promoted to brigadier general, he was sent to Kentucky where his neurotic, volatile temperament and penchant for alarmist dispatches cost him his command and produced reports in the press that he was insane. He turned up next at Shiloh where, having announced minutes before his division was overrun that the nearest Confederate soldier was fifteen miles away, he helped win the battle with a splendid display of combat leadership. Shiloh also cemented his friendship with Grant, with whom he had already established what was probably the most effective working relationship to exist between two generals (not excluding Lee and Jackson) during the war.

In December, 1862, Sherman, by then a major general, was repulsed in an attack on Chickasaw Bluffs, on the Mississippi River, but played a key role in the capture of Vicksburg the following July. In November he led a corps at Missionary Ridge, near Chattanooga, and was fought to a bloody standstill by Pat Cleburne. When Grant was made general-in-chief of the Federal armies and went east in March, 1864, Sherman became supreme commander in the West. Two months later he launched his brilliant campaign in North Georgia, methodically flanking and maneuvering Johnston out of his defensive positions and, ultimately, his job. Except for a frontal attack on Johnston at Kennesaw Mountain that resulted in 2,500 unnecessary casualties, the campaign was a model of judicious use of military power against a numerically inferior opponent. Atlanta fell on September 2. On November

15, after resting his army and dallying briefly with Hood, Sherman abandoned his line of communications to Tennessee and set off in the general direction of the Atlantic Ocean. His intention during the coming campaign, as he put it with characteristic verve and succinctness, was to "make Georgia howl." Behind him, the burning city of Atlanta was howling already.

Sherman's "March to the Sea" introduced an ungrateful world to "Total War" — an improved version of an ancient concept known as "Scorched Earth" and, it is generally believed, Sherman's invention. Sherman's theory was metaphysically sound, paradoxically humane, and, as events proved, effective: The South would be defeated as bloodlessly as possible by destroying its warmaking capacity and breaking the will of its people. Such a course would by definition involve great destruction of property and certain brutalities, but, as Sherman pointed out, destruction of property was better than killing. As for brutalities, his army would be living off the land, and the devastating effects of its passage on the civilian population would in any case be unavoidable. In the probably not quite sincere hope of moderating those effects, or at least the criticism he would receive for causing them, Sherman issued strict orders to control foraging. However, excesses proved to be the rule rather than the exception. Indiscriminate looting and burning were commonplace, and when Sherman reached Savannah at Christmas in 1864 he left behind a smoldering corridor of ruin more than forty miles wide.

After resting and reprovisioning his army at Savannah, Sherman moved into South Carolina in late January, 1865, with the expressed intention of "punishing" the Gamecock State "as she deserves." True to his word, the scourging of the "Cradle of Rebellion" was, if anything, more fearful than that inflicted upon Georgia. The hated foragers, called "bummers," plundered, wrecked, and torched virtually without restraint. The low point came on the night of February 17 when, during a drunken saturnalia, almost half of Columbia was burned to the ground.

With South Carolina ravished and prostrate, Sherman crossed into North Carolina and advanced with his army through the pine woods and up the muddy roads toward Fayetteville. Still only 45 years old, he was now a victorious, decisive, confident general, at the height of his powers — far removed from the mercurial if not mentally unbalanced officer he had seemingly been in 1861 and 1862. Many things had happened in Georgia and South Carolina that he had not ordered or wished, but he felt no regrets. "War is cruelty," he had said, summing up his philosophy. "You cannot refine it. The crueler it is, the sooner it will be over."

FORAGER OR "BUMMER" RETURNING TO CAMP

COLUMBIA IN FLAMES, FEBRUARY 17, 1865

UNITED STATES ARSENAL AT FAYETTEVILLE

—4—

The Armies

On March 11 Sherman's army occupied Fayetteville, where it pillaged dozens of private residences and set fire to factories, banks, mills, tanneries, warehouses, three newspaper offices, all railroad property, and the former U.S. arsenal. On March 14 the Federals moved out again in two 26,000-man columns, one feinting in the direction of Raleigh and the other moving towards Sherman's true goal, Goldsboro. There he planned to link up with the victorious Federal forces marching westward from the North Carolina coast and obtain badly needed supplies.

Sherman's Goldsboro (eastern) column was composed almost entirely of Midwesterners, farm boys from Indiana, Iowa, Illinois, and Ohio with somewhat smaller contingents from Michigan, Missouri, Wisconsin, and Minnesota. Their commander was Oliver O. Howard, a 34-year-old Maine abolitionist who had lost an arm at Seven Pines and was known as "Old Prayer Book" for his piety. The Raleigh column was under 37-year-old New Yorker Henry W. Slocum, who had been wounded in the thigh at First Manassas and defended Culp's Hill at Gettysburg. Slocum's doughty veterans, too, were primarily Midwesterners but with a considerable admixture of men from New York, New Jersey, Pennsylvania, Massachusetts, and Connecticut. The soldiers who trudged northeast from Fayetteville were lean and battle-hardened, but they were road-weary after their seven-week march from Savannah. All looked forward to reaching Goldsboro, where mail, new shoes and uniforms, and other luxuries and necessities would be waiting.

The Confederate Army of Joe Johnston was still massing at Smithfield, about equidistant between Raleigh and Goldsboro. By the time it took the field it would number about 19,000 men, but for now Johnston was still trying to gather its various elements. One 4,500-man component was Johnston's shattered former command, the Army of Tennessee, which was in the middle of an astonishing six-week odyssey from Mississippi over the Confederacy's collapsing railroads. Men from Georgia, Alabama, Mississippi, and Arkansas dominated this decimated but unbowed army, elements of which were still sufficiently buoyant to sing "The Yellow Rose of Texas" while marching with a "jaunty" gait through the streets of Chester, South Carolina, a few weeks earlier. Their commander at Bentonville would be Alexander P. Stewart, a somewhat nondescript 43-year-old Tennesseean known to his men as "Old Strait," who had made a solid if unspectacular reputation during a long career in the West.

The second major element of Johnston's army was a makeshift, 5,400-man force containing a few veteran infantry units, a number of cannonless heavy artillery regiments, and some reserve outfits whose members, for reasons of infirmity, youth, or age, were less than ideal soldier material. Their commander was William J. Hardee, a 49-year-old Georgian who had established himself in North Georgia and on other fields as one of the Confederacy's best corps commanders. Hardee's jackleg force, mustered to offer a minimal resistance to Sherman during the latter stages of his "March to the Sea," had barely managed to elude entrapment at Savannah. It had then retreated across South Carolina without significantly impeding the Federals' progress, picking up the Charleston garrison en route. Almost all of the men were from South Carolina and Georgia. Fearful of what had befallen the families they had left behind at the mercy of Sherman's bummers, they were deserting in alarming numbers to go home and find out for themselves.

The third element of Johnston's command was a 5,500-man force under Braxton Bragg consisting primarily of the division of Robert F. Hoke but also including three recently acquired regiments of North Carolina Junior Reserves — 17-year-olds with minimal combat experience. Hoke's men, most of whom were from North Carolina and Georgia, had been in the Wilmington area when Fort Fisher was captured in January but had been unable to assist their beleaguered compatriots in its defense. Earlier, they had distinguished themselves during the recapture of Plymouth, North Carolina, and had suffered heavy casualties during Lee's dogged defense of Richmond and Petersburg in 1864. After the fall of Wilmington they had retreated to Kinston, where they fought a delaying action against the Federal army of General John Schofield advancing from the North Carolina coast. Bragg, Hoke's superior since Fort Fisher, was probably one of the least capable generals produced by the Confederacy and certainly the most despised — by his soldiers for his brutal discipline and by almost everyone else for his petulant, querulous personality. His inability to command the respect and confidence of his lieutenants and men was sufficient to negate whatever virtues he possessed as an officer and all but destroy his effectiveness as a commander. During the forthcoming battle his presence would be, as it had been on many other fields, a liability.

In addition to the infantry of Stewart, Hardee, and Bragg, Johnston's command included 4,200 cavalrymen ably led by South Carolina aristocrat Wade Hampton and hard-riding young Joe Wheeler. A few of these versatile, reckless horsemen had fought in Virginia and points north during the glory days of dashing "Jeb" Stuart. "I'd rather die than be whipped," Stuart had said on the day he received his death wound. At Bentonville, these survivors of the ride around McClellan's army and their cohorts from other commands, now badly mounted and much reduced by attrition, would fight one last time as though they remembered Stuart's words.

MAJOR GENERAL OLIVER O. HOWARD, U.S.A.

MAJOR GENERAL HENRY W. SLOCUM, U.S.A.

LIEUTENANT GENERAL ALEX. P. STEWART, C.S.A.

LIEUTENANT GENERAL W. J. HARDEE, C.S.A.

GENERAL BRAXTON BRAGG, C.S.A.

MAJOR GENERAL R. F. HOKE, C.S.A.

LIEUTENANT GENERAL WADE HAMPTON, C.S.A.

MAJOR GENERAL JOSEPH WHEELER, C.S.A.

GUARDING FEDERAL ARMY SUPPLIES AT FORT FISHER, NORTH CAROLINA.

THE CAPTURE OF FORT FISHER, JANUARY 15, 1865. *Harper's Weekly*, February 4, 1865.

VIEW OF GOLDSBORO, NORTH CAROLINA. FROM A WAR-TIME SKETCH.

THE FOURTEENTH CORPS ENTERING FAYETTEVILLE. FROM A SKETCH MADE AT THE TIME.

MARCH 16, 1865 — THE BATTLE OF AVERASBORO. *Harper's Weekly*, April 15, 1865.

—5—

Averasboro — Battle in the Mire

As usual, the weather was unsuitable for soldiering. Heavy rains fell, rivers were high or flooding, and glutinous mud was everywhere. None of this had much discernible effect on Sherman, who seemed able to campaign in all climates, seasons, and conditions. True, he had the finest engineers yet seen on the North American continent —men who reputedly would have laid a corduroy turnpike across hell if "Cump," as Sherman's friends called him, had ordered it. However, even terrestrial roads required a little time, and time was one of the things Johnston needed. First, he had to strike before Sherman joined forces with Schofield. Second, Hardee's command and some elements of the Army of Tennessee had not arrived. And third, Johnston's only hope of victory was to destroy one of Sherman's columns before the other could come to its rescue. As it happened, Johnston was to get rain by the barrel, but the resulting sea of mud would delay his operations as much as Sherman's and cost him more.

In addition to time, Johnston also needed information. Was Sherman headed for Goldsboro or Raleigh? Not both, at any rate. His two columns would then diverge beyond supporting distance of each other. Goldsboro seemed more likely. It was closer to Sherman's coastal supply bases and closer to the advancing army of Schofield. It was also a major railroad junction. Which of the two columns should Johnston attack? The western column, under Slocum, was the obvious choice. If Sherman was heading for Goldsboro and Johnston struck Howard, he would have Slocum coming up on one flank and Schofield on the other. He might also be cut off from his line of retreat to Raleigh. On the other hand, if he attacked Slocum he would have Howard and Schofield on his eastern flank, and, if defeated, could fall back to the west in relative safety. Acting under general instructions from Johnston to "impede" Slocum's progress, Hardee decided to obtain some of the information and time the Confederates needed by digging in his tatterdemalion command and offering battle.

"Old Reliable," as Hardee was known, chose his ground with the care to be expected of a general who was outnumbered on the order of four- or five-to-one. In fact, the spot he chose was not so much "ground" as a swamp. Two rivers, the Cape Fear and the Black, protected the Confederates' flanks, and creeks, bogs, ravines, and heavy underbrush guarded parts of their front. In some places the field was knee-deep in water. Then it began to rain. Well aware of the shakiness of some of his inexperienced troops, Hardee established three defensive lines with the least reliable units to the front. There, knowing that if forced to retreat they would be falling back on seasoned veterans, they might put up a stiffer fight.

Skirmishing began on the afternoon of March 15 as Slocum's advance guard stumbled onto Hardee's pickets. The next morning the Federals, "encased in an armor of mud," routed part of the Charleston garrison from Hardee's first line. The second line was pierced with even less difficulty that afternoon. Storming ahead, the Federals were precariously halted by the third line until darkness fell. During the night the Confederates received orders to build fires as if going into camp and then "get down, stooping, or on all fours, and withdraw, not speaking above a whisper." While the bullets of Federal sharpshooters plinked bark and needles from the pine trees overhead, Hardee's troops silently fell back. "We plodded all night," a South Carolinian recalled, "all day on Friday, camped on Friday night in the piny woods, and then went on to a place called Elevation by noon on Saturday (March 18). From Thursday till midday Saturday we were without any rations save a very small slice of raw bacon to each man. Our entire march from Charleston was hard, but the tramp from Averasboro to Elevation was the worst of the whole stretch." Casualties in Hardee's command at Averasboro numbered about 500 men killed, wounded, captured, and missing. The Federals reported their losses at 678.

Although Averasboro was a defeat for Hardee in a conventional sense, it accomplished everything he wanted and more. So confident was Sherman that he had not even halted Howard's advance while Slocum was engaged at Averasboro. In addition to increasing the distance between the two columns, this strongly suggested that Sherman either had no idea of the Confederate concentration at Smithfield or had badly underestimated its strength. It also suggested, and was to be confirmed in a matter of hours, that Sherman's destination was Goldsboro. Thus Johnston could now forget about protecting Raleigh and offer battle in the certainty that Slocum would come to him. Clearly, the moment to strike had arrived. Johnston began moving his army south toward Bentonville and ordered Hardee to join him there. By sunrise on March 19 most of Johnston's men were in place. Hardee was still six miles away but had been on the march over muddy roads since 4:00 A.M. that morning.

CONFEDERATES MOVING GUNS ON A CORDUROY ROAD.

ADVANCING UNDER DIFFICULTIES.

—6—

Sunrise, March 19, 1865

The day dawned clear and "balmy." Apple and peach trees bloomed here and there, blending harmoniously with the delicate spring foliage of red maples and the deeper hues of loblolly pines. Slocum's men sat around campfires finishing their Sunday breakfasts and listening to the familiar notes of a favorite hymn, "Old Hundredth," played by a brigade band. There had been fighting the previous day as Hampton's cavalry slashed and parried with Slocum's advance guard, narrowly preventing it from occupying the ground chosen for Johnston's ambush. Hampton's horsemen had seemed more determined than usual, peppering their opponents with rifle fire from every patch of woods and crossroads, but most of the Federal generals, including Sherman, were unperturbed. Several reports regarding Johnston's whereabouts, line of retreat, and probable intentions had reached Sherman within the past few hours. None gave any cause for alarm. In fact, the Federal commander had already delivered himself of two Shiloh-like pearls of wisdom to allay the fears of his more apprehensive lieutenants. "They won't fight us this side of Smithfield or Raleigh," he told one. "Brush them out of the way," he ordered another. "There is nothing there but cavalry." With that he rode off with a small escort to join Howard and the right wing.

Sherman's ride to join Howard that morning was shorter than Johnston had hoped — six miles at most, probably less. However, Howard's column was floundering over muddy roads and badly strung out. Slocum was in even worse shape. The two Fourteenth Corps divisions from which Sherman took his departure, commanded by Generals W. P. Carlin and J. D. Morgan, constituted less than half of Slocum's strength.* They were also about eight miles ahead of two sister divisions from the Twentieth Corps that very shortly would attempt to come to their rescue. Howard was closer but, incredibly, was already passing out of the picture. While the left wing was fighting for its life on the 19th, Howard, acting on Sherman's orders and reassured by a misguided message from Slocum, marched steadily away from the battle.

The first signs of trouble came with a clatter of rifle fire from the foragers, who had set out on their daily expedition at about 5:00 A.M. Scarcely a mile up the Goldsboro road they had run into Hampton's pickets, who were closer to the Federal camp than they had ever been and full of fight. One foraging party, startled by the accidental discovery that Confederate infantry were entrenching in large numbers along Slocum's line of march, sent back a warning, but the rider never reached his destination.

*The four corps of Sherman's army averaged about 13,000 men. The strength of divisions and brigades varied considerably but averaged about 3,700 and 1,300 men respectively. The number of men in equivalent units of Johnston's army varied so widely as to make averages largely meaningless. For purposes of this account, it is worth noting that the strength of Hoke's division was about 4,800 men, that of Taliaferro about 2,000 men, and that of McLaws about 3,200 men.

While the Federals finished their hardtack and coffee, Johnston deployed his army. The Confederate line began south of the Goldsboro road, crossed it near its intersection with the western branch of the road leading north to Bentonville, then bent back about forty-five degrees before making a long right angle zag to the west — thereby giving the position a sickle-like configuration. South of the Goldsboro road the line extended through dense, marshy blackjack thickets that severely limited visibility and movement; north of the road, concealed just inside the fringe of a woods, it followed the eastern and northern contours of a field belonging to a hardscrabble planter named Cole. Cole's modest house was situated just north of the road at a point a few hundred yards west of the nearest Confederate position.

Hoke's division, including the brigade of North Carolina Junior Reserves, under Bragg, manned the Confederate works from their southern extremity to a point a half mile north of the Goldsboro road. Hardee's force was supposed to hold the center but, thanks to faulty maps and the mud, had not yet arrived from Elevation. In its absence, two batteries of horse artillery were inserted into the gap. Beyond Hardee's position, concealed along the northern edge of the woods, was Stewart's Army of Tennessee. Johnston's plan was simple. Hampton would delay Slocum's advance as long as possible, thereby giving Hardee time to reach the field. Johnston would then bring Slocum to a bloody halt on the anvil of Bragg's command before smashing him with a devastating hammer blow from Hardee and Stewart. It was a good plan, worthy of one of the Confederacy's best tacticians. Except for the absence of Hardee, the circumstances and elements Johnston needed for victory seemed to be in place.

WOUNDED AND STRAGGLERS ON THE WAY TO THE REAR AND AMMUNITION WAGONS GOING TO THE FRONT.

—7—

Ambush

Up the Goldsboro road the rattle of rifle fire rose to new levels as Carlin's division moved out at 7:00 A.M. The foragers were making no progress, and the skirmishers who now joined them seemed to be merely adding to the din. Increasingly suspicious, Carlin deployed his three brigades and ordered them forward to probe the Confederate position. Part of the first brigade, under Harrison Hobart, had reached the Cole house when Hoke unleashed a blast of musket and artillery fire, sending the Federals scrambling for the cover of a wooded ravine. The second brigade, under G. P. Buell, moving on Hobart's left and now diverging rapidly from it, was ordered to fall back quickly to link up with Hobart. South of the road, the remainder of Hobart's brigade and the third brigade, commanded by David Miles, halted to await instructions. Artillery fire continued to rain down on the position of Hobart and Buell, and the Confederates also began to take casualties as Federal artillery reached the field and opened up on Hoke.

With Buell in position on Hobart's left, Carlin ordered his command forward again. North of the road Hobart and Buell, in the mistaken belief that they were flanking Hoke, unexpectedly plowed into the Army of Tennessee and were received with a "sheet of fire" from a distance of about fifty feet.

> They . . . reeled and staggered [one Confederate reported] while we poured volley after volley into them, and great gaps were made in their line, as brave Federals fell everywhere — their colors would rise and fall just a few feet from us, and many a gallant boy in blue is buried there in those pines who held "Old Glory" up for a brief moment.

"We went for them with a yell," one Federal officer wrote home a few days later. "I tell you it was a tight place. . . . We stood as long as man can stand and . . . [then] run like the deuce." South of the road, Miles attacked "again and again" but was beaten off by Hoke's sturdy veterans. Taking alarm at the fierceness and persistence of the Federal assaults and fearing that Hoke was about to be overwhelmed, Bragg called on Johnston for reinforcements. "Most injudiciously," as Johnston later put it, he (Johnston) diverted the division of Lafayette McLaws, the first of Hardee's units to reach the field, from its assigned position in the Confederate center, thereby delaying and weakening Johnston's planned counterattack. By the time McLaws made his way through the tangled woods to Hoke, Miles had been repulsed. Now was the moment for Johnston to deliver his hammer blow from the north, but Hardee's force was still coming up. Johnston decided to wait.

At about this time, a key event in the Battle of Bentonville took place. As Carlin's battered brigades fell back, three Confederate deserters — former Federal soldiers who had been captured and had enlisted in the Confederate Army rather than face starvation in a prison camp — made a dash for the Federal lines. With them they brought the information that Johnston was on the field with the largest Confederate army Sherman had seen since he left Atlanta. This news was received by Slocum with extreme skepticism until an aide recognized one of the deserters as a fellow townsman from Syracuse, New York. Quickly, Slocum dispatched a courier to Sherman with news of the true situation at Bentonville. Word was also sent to the Twentieth Corps, still six miles or so from the battlefield, to hasten to the scene.

While these events were taking place, Morgan's 4,700-man division of the Fourteenth Corps arrived and was dispatched south of the Goldsboro road to the support of Miles, whose line was thereby extended to the right. One of Morgan's brigades, under B. D. Fearing, was placed in reserve behind Miles. Heavy skirmishing continued up and down the lines, but Morgan found himself under no particular pressure and set to work fortifying his position. Having no entrenching tools at hand, the men felled trees with hatchets and in about two hours of feverish effort constructed a formidable log breastwork.

It was now about 2:00 P.M. Hardee's other division, under William B. Taliaferro, began arriving and was dispatched to the far right to extend Stewart's line. The Federals also received reinforcements in the form of a Twentieth Corps brigade commanded by J. S. Robinson, who was ordered to fill the gap in the center of the Federal line between Hobart's right and Miles's left. Having insufficient strength to accomplish that task, Robinson placed part of his unit to the rear of the gap and began entrenching. This work was still in progress when, at 2:45 P.M., Johnston launched his attack.

MAJOR GENERAL LAFAYETTE McLAWS, C.S.A.

KINCHEN JAHU CARPENTER
Twenty-two year old private from Rutherford County.
Served in Company I, 50th Regiment, North Carolina Troops, McLaws's Division
Published with permission of Mrs. D. C. Ward, Lake Lure, NC.

— 8 —

"Some Of The Best Running Ever Did"

Shrieking the Rebel Yell, the Confederate right wing, under Hardee, swept forward. To observers elsewhere on the field, the scene was "like a picture" as the ragged, gray- and butternut-clad Confederates charged through the woods and across the fields "in perfect order" with "colors flying." For probably the first time that day, Federal soldiers in the ranks, who were outnumbered at this point on the order of two to one, realized the strength of their opposition. A blast of fire from the positions of Hobart, Buell, and Robinson staggered the Confederates momentarily, but they came on again. Cheers, screams, curses, and shouts of command rose above the crash of cannon fire and the thunderous roar of thousands of rifles and muskets. Presently, Buell's brigade, seeing Confederates advancing on its unprotected left flank, "broke panic stricken," throwing away guns and knapsacks and "running like a flock of sheep." It was followed moments later by Hobart's brigade and then Robinson's. "As far as the eye could reach," one Federal officer wrote, the rebel regiments came on, "advancing rapidly and firing as they came.... The onward sweep of the rebel lines was like the waves of the ocean, resistless."

While the fugitives from the commands of Buell, Hobart, and Robinson fled westward through the fields and woods — demonstrating to "the Rebs as well as the outside," in the words of one of them, "some of the best running ever did" — Morgan's men hunkered down in their log fort and prepared to fight for their lives. Hardee paused briefly to re-form his line and send Taliaferro's division and the corps of W. B. Bate in pursuit of Carlin, then surged forward again. With the Confederate avalanche roaring down on their flank and rear and minie balls "whizzing in every direction," Miles's brigade and part of Hobart's brigade were driven into a swamp, where they remained inactive for the rest of the day. The reserve brigade of Fearing then pitched into Hardee's flank, screaming "We'll whip them yet" and momentarily halting the stunned Confederates in their tracks. Fearing's men were swept aside after a sharp fight, but Hardee was again forced to pause and redeploy. This further delayed the attack on Morgan and bought some time for the demolished Federal left, which was attempting to rally on a newly arrived division of the Twentieth Corps a mile and a half away down the Goldsboro road.

By now it was 4:30 P.M. Hoke's division, which remained idle under orders from Bragg during Hardee's assaults, at last got into the fight by attacking Morgan from the front. Relatively fresh and unbloodied amid the carnage that had been taking place around them, Morgan's men were ready. Instead of attacking as Hoke wished through the gap created by the withdrawal of Fearing, Bragg ordered a frontal assault through the thickets and swamps against Morgan's bristling hedgehog fortifications. Battling desperately amid a "continuous and remorseless roar of musketry," Morgan's men narrowly held their ground, beating back the charging Confederates with heavy casualties. Hardee then advanced again, a trifle too late to coordinate his attack with that of Hoke. With the corps of D. H. Hill in the lead, the Confederates fell upon Morgan's rear. Morgan's men, fighting now from the opposite side of their works, received Hill with a full-face blast of musketry that knocked the Confederates reeling. A few minutes later a brigade of the Twentieth Corps, arriving on the field after an eight-mile double-quick, struck the battered and frazzled Confederates from behind, sending most of them scrambling back to the Goldsboro road. Others, surrounded, attempted to defend themselves from a hollow square. Those who were "fleet of foot" or who hid themselves until dark in the "thick gallberry bushes" escaped; the remainder were killed or captured.

While Hardee and Hoke had been pounding away at the lethal hornet's nest devised by Morgan, the Federal left had been rebuilt and fortified by units of Alpheus Williams's Twentieth Corps, bolstered by the survivors of Carlin's division. Taking full advantage of an hour-long respite between the rout of Carlin and the renewal of the Confederate assault on the left, Williams had prepared a hornet's nest of his own. Working in two shifts, during which half of his men wielded axes and spades at a frantic pace for a few minutes and were then replaced by the other half, the Federals quickly constructed "a splendid set of works." A four-hundred-yard gap existed in the middle of the Federal line, but this was covered by twenty-six cannon with a clear field of fire. An attack on this position would be costly under any circumstances and suicidal unless the assault force held a decisive numerical advantage.

At about 5:30 P.M. Taliaferro's division launched a series of attacks against the Twentieth Corps. Each of these was received, according to one South Carolinian, by a "raging leaden hailstorm of grape and canister" that lopped limbs off trees and stripped them of their bark. Every available Federal was placed in the line, including the headquarters guard. Artillery ordnance was fired off by the wagon load as the cannoneers double-shotted their guns and packed handfuls of bullets down on top of shells. "The onset [attack] was the most desperate of the war," one Federal wrote. "Column followed column in succession . . . to carry our position at any cost." Heavy and confused fighting continued until well after dark. "So close and murderous was this combat," another Federal recalled, "that piles of 'Rebs' lay dead within our lines and around the general's [Williams] headquarters." The Federals watched the survivors of this last attack fall back with deep relief. During the course of the slaughter they had used up almost all of their ammunition.

Several hours later, at about 9:30 P.M., word of the heavy fighting and near disaster at Bentonville was delivered to Sherman.

MARCH 19-21, 1865 — THE BATTLE OF BENTONVILLE. *Harper's Weekly*, April 15, 1865.

— 9 —

Night of Anguish

Slocum's message describing the true situation at Bentonville reached Sherman at a place called Falling Creek Church, about twenty miles from the battlefield. Dressed in a red flannel undershirt and drawers, he erupted from a tent and, standing in the ankle-deep ashes of a camp fire, began barking orders. Concentric rings of frantic activity quickly spread through Howard's command. His column was still badly strung out, so the distances his various units would have to cover varied considerably. By hard marching most of them could reach Bentonville by midafternoon. In one sense, the column's lack of compactness was an advantage: the men would arrive more quickly because they would not all be moving over the same road until their routes converged northeast of the battlefield. At that point they would be advancing down the Goldsboro road directly into Hoke's rear. Johnston would either have to re-form his lines and fight twice the numbers he had faced on the 19th or retreat in a hurry.

At Bentonville, a night of anguish was passing. About a mile behind Williams's position, at the home of John Harper, a prosperous farmer, Federal surgeons were busy bandaging wounds and sawing off arms and legs, which they unceremoniously tossed out the windows. Up the Goldsboro road their Confederate counterparts were similarly engaged. The field was littered with those who were forever beyond earthly help. Some, killed by artillery fire, were dismembered, or half-stripped and flayed; others, felled by minie balls, lay more peacefully, seemingly uninjured. Among the dead were scores of wounded who could not be reached by litter parties or who were too severely injured to drag themselves to safety. Some lay silently; others groaned, whimpered, or called for help. The cries of one wounded Confederate were so pitiful that they roused an entire Ohio regiment, but a would-be rescuer was turned back by his own pickets. Around the battlefield, dozens of small fires smoldered in stumps and thickets, covering the area with a pall of acrid smoke. Cannon boomed from time to time, causing a few additional casualties and preventing the exhausted soldiers from building campfires around which to cook, dry clothes, or obtain warmth. Those who were able slept fitfully on their arms. Lightning shimmered on the northeast horizon, fog rolled in, and in the flooded marshes near Morgan's position some desperately wounded men probably drowned in a few inches of water.

During the night the two armies adjusted their lines and improved their fortifications. Johnston withdrew his right wing to the position it had occupied that morning. Both armies were resupplied with ammunition. At about sunrise the first division of reinforcements from Howard's command, coming down the Goldsboro road behind Hoke, encountered Confederate pickets. While Wheeler's cavalry fought a delaying action, Hoke redeployed north of the road with his left flank bent back sharply on a north-south axis. Thus Johnston's line now took on the shape of a spraddled horseshoe with both flanks resting on Mill Creek. This new position, although undoubtedly the only one possible, had two flaws that were potentially fatal. First, Johnston's force was too small to man it properly, so that long stretches of both flanks were protected only by dismounted cavalry; and second, the only withdrawal route was over a narrow bridge spanning Mill Creek. To remain at Bentonville one minute longer than necessary was to court disaster. Sherman was certain that Johnston, now heavily outnumbered by a united Federal army, would quickly get his command out of harm's way —probably during the night of the 20th. Once again, he was wrong.

MARCH 21, 1865 — THE IMPROMPTU CHARGE OF GENERAL J. A. MOWER ON THE CONFEDERATE FLANK AT BENTONVILLE.
(From *The Soldier in Our Civil War*)

— 10 —

Death of a Boy Soldier

While Johnston repositioned his lines during the early morning hours of March 20, fresh units from Howard's column continued to arrive. By late afternoon most of Howard's command was in place on the Federal right. Fighting flared briefly around 10 A.M. when a probing attack by Morgan was shot to pieces by one of Hoke's North Carolina brigades firing by ranks — two lines of men alternately firing their weapons and lying down to reload. "[We] mowed [them] down," one North Carolinian recalled, "like wheat before the scythe." Heavy skirmishing took place elsewhere on the field, but in comparison with the events of the 19th the day passed quietly. Confederate ambulances rolled north over the Mill Creek bridge in the direction of Smithfield, but a shortage of vehicles and the condition of the roads created major difficulties. At nightfall the evacuation of the wounded was still in progress with no prospect of finishing the task before morning. Johnston was determined not to leave these men behind. He decided to remain at Bentonville another day, even in the face of Sherman's reunited army.

For his part, Sherman was puzzled and apprehensive. He could see no reason for Johnston to hold his ground. Was he stronger than Sherman thought? Was he expecting reinforcements? These concerns were genuine but also largely irrelevant. Even were Johnston's army twice its actual size, it would not pose a serious threat. In any case Sherman had no intention of taking the offensive. Only rarely had he expended lives in attack when maneuver would accomplish his object, and he saw no reason to do so now that the war was clearly nearing its end. Goldsboro was his goal, and he intended to get there as speedily as possible. As had been the case at Averasboro, he seemed almost indifferent to the matter at hand. An opportunity to obliterate one of the two major Confederate armies still in the field was thus lost; but, in a larger sense, Sherman's judgment was sound. The war would end in any case in a few weeks, and hundreds of men from both armies would live to rear families and prosper who otherwise would have died at Bentonville.

If Sherman did not want to fight, one Federal general did. Looking across the field from his position on the Federal right on the afternoon of the 21st, Joseph A. Mower, whom Sherman had once described as "the boldest young soldier we have," chaffed and fumed, his martial ardor undampened by the cold rain that was dampening everyone else's. Here, it seemed, was a victory for the taking. What could Sherman be waiting for? Skirmishing continued at various points along the line, raising Mower's hopes for an attack, but still Sherman did not move. Finally, Mower could stand it no longer. On his own initiative he ordered his division to attack and seize the Mill Creek bridge.

Sweeping aside a line of dismounted cavalry and driving past a field hospital, whose ambulatory patients made off as fast as their injuries permitted, Mower's division barreled deep into the Confederate rear. Confederate reinforcements were ordered to the scene, but it was clear they could not arrive in time to save the bridge and Johnston's army. Abruptly, eighty members of the Eighth Texas Cavalry Regiment, "holding their bridle reins in their mouths and a pistol in each hand," pitched into Mower's left flank. At the same time, a cavalry brigade under Hampton attacked from the right, a brigade of Georgia infantry from McLaws's division opened up on the Federals from the front, and 500 Alabama cavalrymen under Wheeler came in on Mower's rear. The violence and determination of these weak but coordinated assaults, together with a peremptory message from Sherman to return to his lines, brought the impetuous young general up short. His men were only about 200 yards from Johnston's headquarters and about 300 short of the main road leading to the bridge over Mill Creek.

For Hardee, who conducted the defense of the Confederate left, a moment of genuine if essentially barren triumph turned quickly to despair when two litter-bearers trudged by bearing his badly wounded son Willie, aged sixteen. Willie's war had been short. After several years of protective exile at a Georgia military school, the impatient young warrior had been allowed to join his father. Only a few hours earlier he had been sworn in, with Hardee's reluctant permission, as a member of the Eighth Texas Cavalry. Now he had been shot down during the repulse of Mower in a forlorn-hope charge that General Hardee himself had led. Hardee dismounted and went over to his only son for a few moments, then sadly rode off with Hampton. Willie was removed in an ambulance to Hillsborough, about seventy-five miles to the northwest, to be cared for by his stepmother and sister. There he died on March 24 with his father at his side and was buried, after the military funeral he would have wanted, in the churchyard of St. Matthew's Episcopal Church. Among those who mourned the news of his death was Oliver O. Howard, one of Mower's superior officers. Some years earlier, when General Hardee had been superintendent of the military academy at West Point and Howard had been a professor, "Old Prayer Book" had been Willie's tutor and Sunday School teacher.

MAJOR GENERAL J. A. MOWER, U.S.A.

GRAVE MARKER OF WILLIE HARDEE IN ST. MATTHEW'S EPISCOPAL CHURCH CEMETERY, HILLSBOROUGH. CONTRARY TO THE MARKER, YOUNG HARDEE WAS ONLY SIXTEEN YEARS OLD WHEN HE DIED OF WOUNDS RECEIVED AT BENTONVILLE. THE CORRECT DATE OF HIS DEATH IS BELIEVED TO BE MARCH 24, 1865.

BENTONVILLE THE MORNING AFTER THE BATTLE — THE SMOKE IS FROM RESIN THAT WAS FIRED BY THE CONFEDERATES. FROM A SKETCH MADE AT THE TIME.

JAMES BENNITT'S HOUSE, WHERE JOHNSTON SURRENDERED

— 11 —

Aftermath

Rain fell again on the night of March 21, turning the heavily wooded banks of Mill Creek and much of the battlefield into a quagmire. Johnston's position was now critical. His troops were cold, wet, hungry, and exhausted, the Mill Creek bridge could be cut at any moment by a sudden Federal lunge, and Schofield's 23,000-man army had reached Goldsboro. This latter development was decisive. Schofield's force alone was larger than Johnston's, and it was at most a two-day march from either Bentonville or Smithfield. Not only was Smithfield Johnston's base, his only withdrawal route led there. Johnston had no choice but to retreat. Leaving only a few of the most critically wounded men behind, his army pulled out during the night of the 21st, crossed the Mill Creek bridge, and headed north. Rain continued to delay the weary Confederates as they floundered through the mud and blackjack thickets in inky darkness. By 8:00 A.M. the rear of Johnston's column was still passing through the town of Bentonville, south of Mill Creek.

Sherman had been aware since dawn of Johnston's withdrawal, and R. F. Catterson's brigade of Howard's Fifteenth Corps was dispatched to speed him on his way. Just south of Bentonville the Federals collided with Wheeler's cavalry, which was covering the retreat. A running fight to Mill Creek ensued as Wheeler battled with "considerable warmth" to fend off Catterson. After scattering Wheeler's dismounted horsemen at the Mill Creek bridge and extinguishing their attempt to burn the structure, Catterson moved rapidly on to the bridge over nearby Hannah Creek. There Wheeler made another, more determined stand, beating back a Federal attack on the bridge and shooting down three color bearers within fifty feet of his line. Catterson then fell back to Mill Creek, putting an end to the fighting on March 22 and to the Battle of Bentonville.

In the context of Civil War history, Bentonville was not a large battle. On March 19, when most of the fighting took place, Johnston had perhaps 19,000 men on the field; Slocum about the same. Federal losses during the three days were 1,527 men killed, wounded, and captured; Confederate casualties have been put at 2,463. It is also clear in retrospect that the Battle of Bentonville, as both Sherman and Johnston seem to have known before it was fought, never had any chance of seriously altering the course of events. Even had Slocum's column been totally destroyed, Johnston would have faced an aroused Sherman with 53,000 men from the combined commands of Howard and Schofield — a force almost as large as the one Sherman had fielded before Bentonville. Grant's victorious army of more than 100,000 men also would soon be ready to take the field in North Carolina. A Rebel victory at Bentonville might have prolonged the war by a few weeks, but it could not have changed its outcome.

All of that notwithstanding, Johnston had done very well. His battle plan had been well-conceived and bold, he had taken Sherman by surprise, and he had contrived to isolate, at least for a day, one wing of the Federal army. Furthermore, his outnumbered and much-defeated soldiers had fought with great valor — as had their Federal counterparts — and unexpected, even extraordinary discipline. All that brave men could do, they did. If Hardee had arrived on time; if McLaws had not been diverted unnecessarily to the assistance of Hoke; and if Morgan had not fortified his position south of the Goldsboro road beyond the requirements of immediate necessity, the result might have been different.

While Johnston's army completed its withdrawal to Smithfield, Sherman moved on to Goldsboro, where his men began arriving on the 23rd. A respite of more than two weeks followed. On April 10, the day after Lee surrendered at Appomattox Court House, Sherman marched out of Goldsboro in the direction of Raleigh, forcing Johnston to evacuate Smithfield. Raleigh was occupied on April 13, and four days later Sherman and Johnston met at the home of James Bennitt, near Durham Station, to discuss surrender terms. These were signed at the same place on April 26, bringing the Civil War in the East, effectively if not quite literally, to a close.

The principal actors in the drama at Bentonville now moved on to other stages to meet their various fates. Mower was dead within five years — of pneumonia — at the age of 42, while Wheeler lived to command American troops more than thirty years later in the Spanish-American War. Johnston was elected to the U.S. House of Representatives for one term in 1879 and later served for six years as commissioner of railroads during the administrations of Grover Cleveland and Benjamin Harrison. His old adversary, Sherman, became commander-in-chief of the U.S. Army in 1869 and was unsuccessfully importuned to run for president on the Republican ticket in 1884. Aphoristic and blunt to the last, he rejected these overtures with what became the classical "Shermanesque" disavowal of many unwilling candidates for public office: "If nominated I will not run, if elected I will not serve." He also gave us "War is Hell," an observation with which many southerners who experienced his passing would have agreed while adding the corollary that "The Devil ought to know." While understandable, this was an injustice to a man whose actions in the South were never motivated by hatred or cruelty and who — a poor performance at Bentonville notwithstanding — was one of America's greatest soldiers.

Sherman died in New York City on February 14, 1891, and was buried in St. Louis. Among the mourners was Joe Johnston, who contracted a cold while marching bareheaded in the funeral procession. Five weeks later he too was dead.

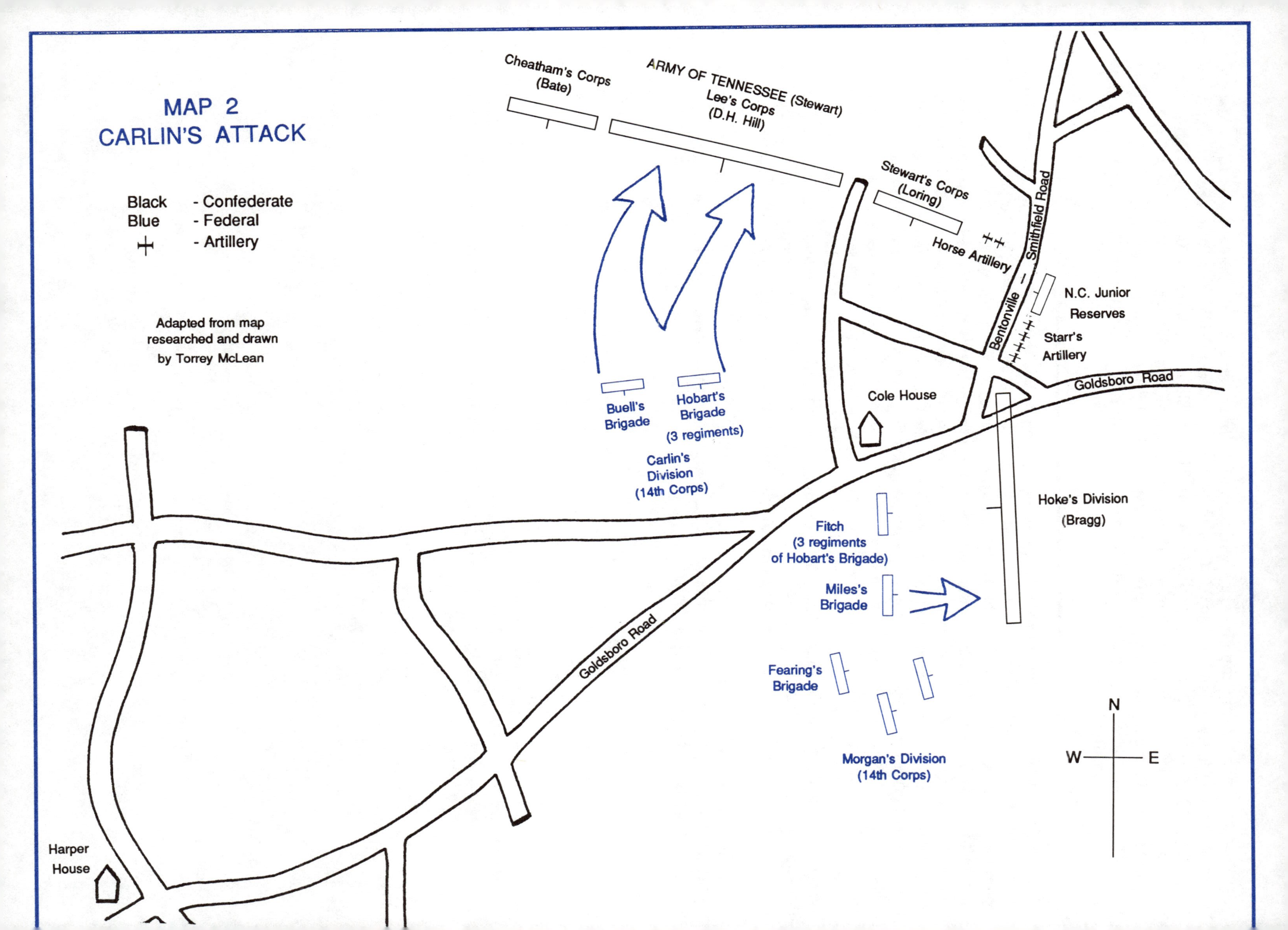
MAP 2
CARLIN'S ATTACK
Black - Confederate
Blue - Federal
- Artillery
Adapted from map
researched and drawn
by Torrey McLean
Cheatham's Corps
(Bate)
ARMY OF TENNESSEE (Stewart)
Lee's Corps
(D.H. Hill)
Stewart's Corps
(Loring)
Horse Artillery
Smithfield Road
Bentonville
N.C. Junior
Reserves
Starr's
Artillery
Goldsboro Road
Cole House
Buell's
Brigade
Hobart's
Brigade
(3 regiments)
Carlin's
Division
(14th Corps)
Hoke's Division
(Bragg)
Fitch
(3 regiments
of Hobart's Brigade)
Miles's
Brigade
Goldsboro Road
Fearing's
Brigade
Morgan's Division
(14th Corps)
N
W
E
Harper
House

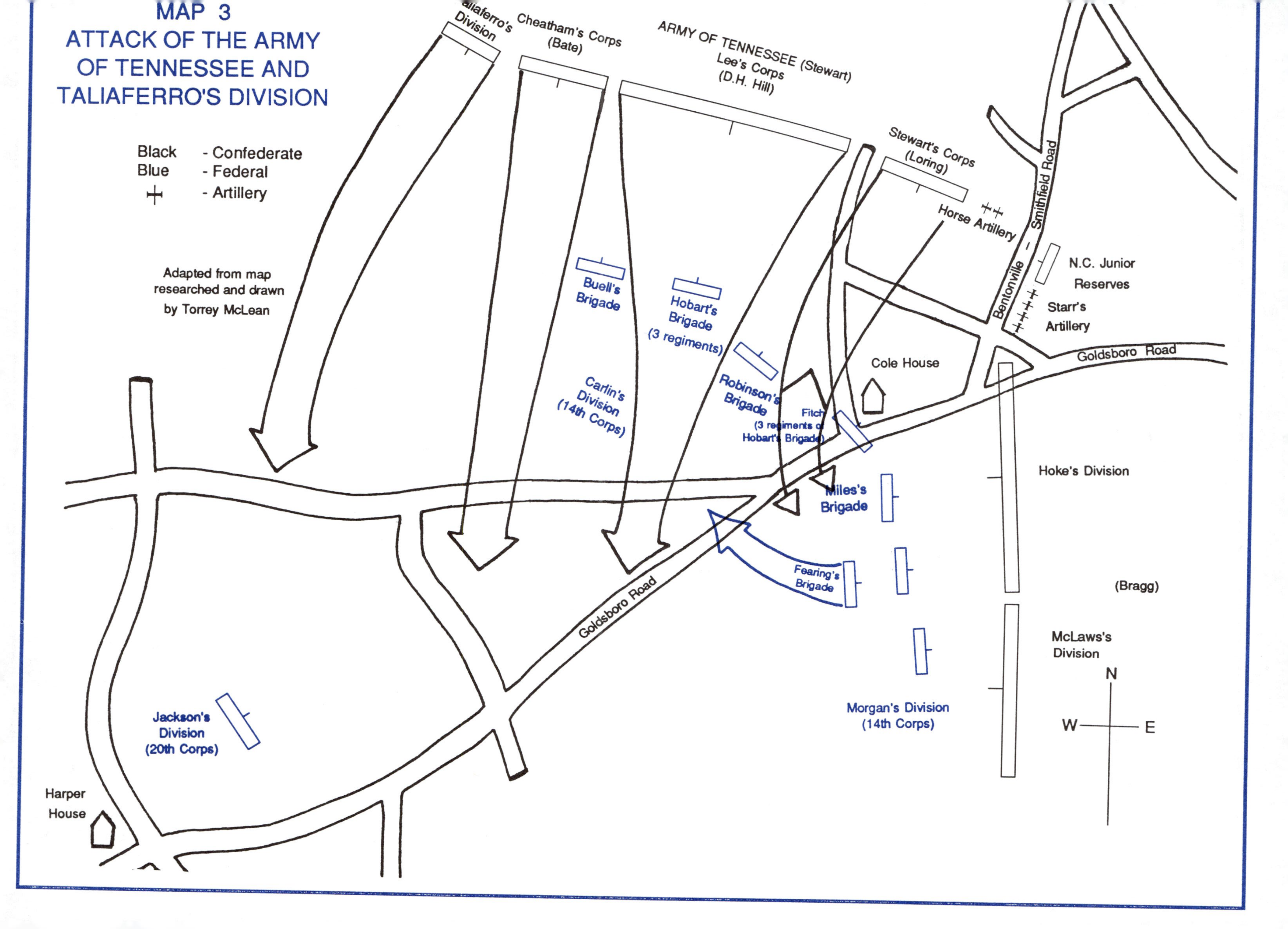
MAP 3
ATTACK OF THE ARMY OF TENNESSEE AND TALIAFERRO'S DIVISION
Black - Confederate
Blue - Federal
- Artillery
Adapted from map researched and drawn by Torrey McLean
aliaferro's Division
Cheatham's Corps (Bate)
ARMY OF TENNESSEE (Stewart)
Lee's Corps (D.H. Hill)
Stewart's Corps (Loring)
Horse Artillery
Smithfield Road
Bentonville
N.C. Junior Reserves
Starr's Artillery
Goldsboro Road
Cole House
Buell's Brigade
Hobart's Brigade (3 regiments)
Robinson's Brigade
Fitch (3 regiments of Hobart's Brigade)
Carlin's Division (14th Corps)
Miles's Brigade
Fearing's Brigade
Hoke's Division
(Bragg)
McLaws's Division
Morgan's Division (14th Corps)
Goldsboro Road
N
W
E
Jackson's Division (20th Corps)
Harper House

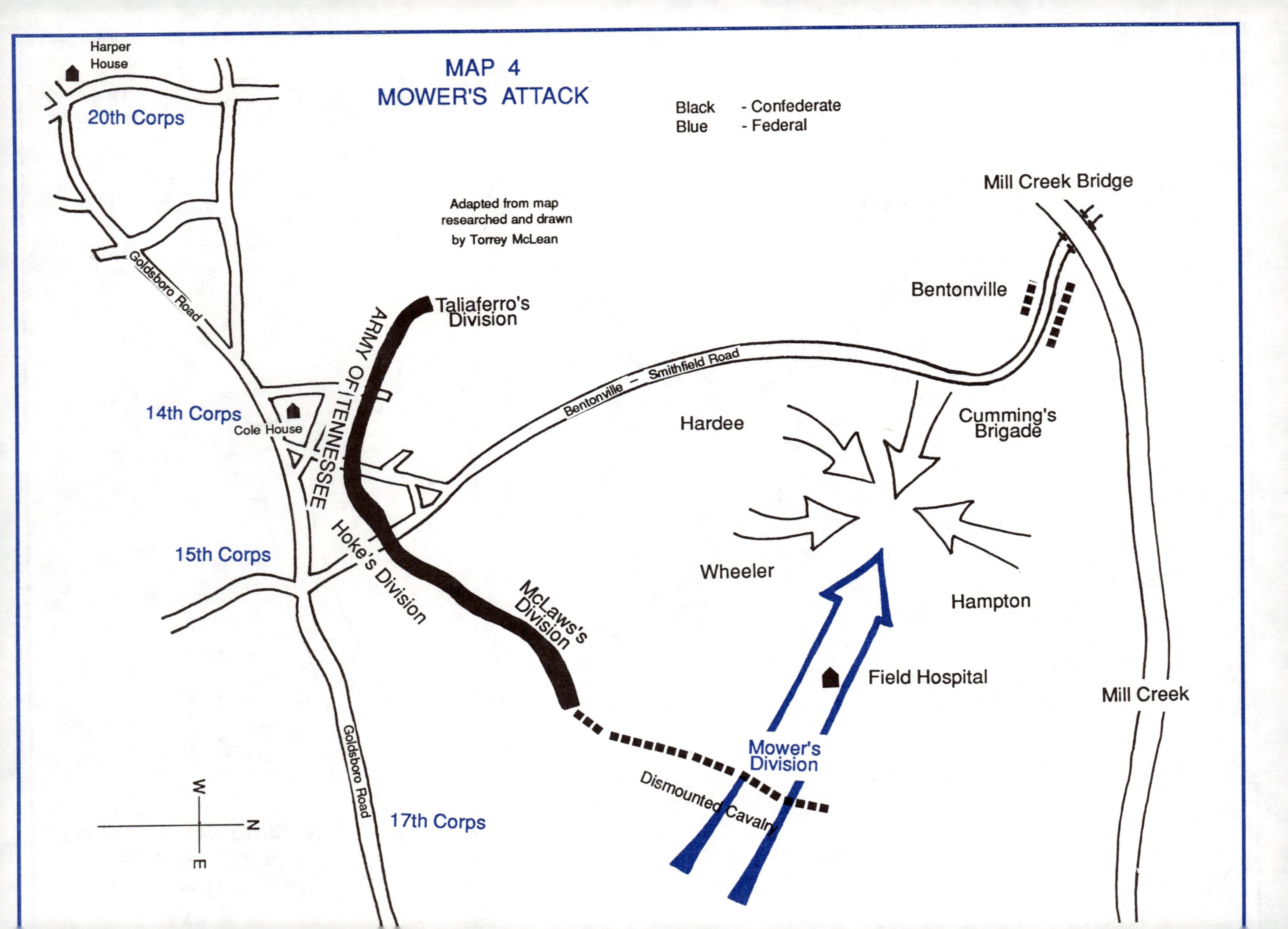
MAP 4
MOWER'S ATTACK
Black - Confederate
Blue - Federal
Adapted from map researched and drawn by Torrey McLean
Harper House
20th Corps
Goldsboro Road
14th Corps
Cole House
15th Corps
17th Corps
ARMY OF TENNESSEE
Taliaferro's Division
Hoke's Division
McLaws's Division
Bentonville – Smithfield Road
Bentonville
Mill Creek Bridge
Mill Creek
Hardee
Cumming's Brigade
Wheeler
Hampton
Field Hospital
Mower's Division
Dismounted Cavalry
N
W
E

BENTONVILLE TODAY.

ENTRANCE TO PARK.

VISITOR'S CENTER.

THE HARPER HOUSE
FOLLOWING THE BATTLE, 45 CONFEDERATE WOUNDED WERE HOSPITALIZED IN THE HARPER HOUSE. NINETEEN OF THESE MEN DIED.

INTERIOR OF HARPER HOUSE.

CONFEDERATE CEMETERY MARKER ERECTED IN 1893.

MONUMENT TO TEXAS CAVALRY.

RECONSTRUCTED FIELD FORTIFICATION.

REMAINS OF UNION TRENCHES.

CAPTURED CONFEDERATE FLAG ON
DISPLAY AT VISITOR'S CENTER

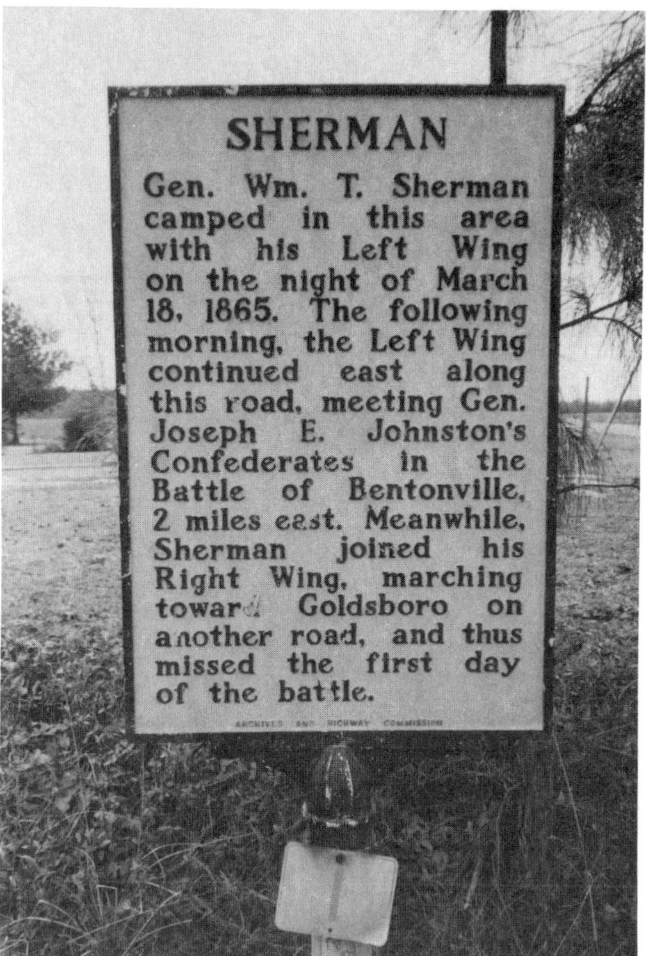

TYPICAL BATTLEFIELD MARKER.

BATTLEGROUND MARKER ERECTED BY U.D.C. IN 1927.

INDEX